Tadpole Books are published by Jump!, 5357 Penn Avenue South, Minneapolis, MN 55419, www.jumplibrary.com

Copyright ©2023 Jump. International copyright reserved in all countries. No part of this book may be reproduced in any form without written permission from the publisher.

Editor: Jenna Gleisner **Designer:** Emma Bersie **Translator:** Annette Granat

Photo Credits: Anatoliy Karlyuk/Shutterstock, cover; Photo Melon/Shutterstock, 1; ABO PHOTOGRAPHY/Shutterstock, 2ml, 8–9; EpicStockMedia/Shutterstock, 2tr, 12–13; wavebreakmedia/Shutterstock, 2mr, 2br, 4–5, 14–15; Hairem/Shutterstock, 2bl, 10–11; clickit/Shutterstock, 2tl, 6–7; PeopleImages/iStock, 3; stockphoto-graf/Shutterstock, 16:1; Utekhina Anna/Shutterstock, 16tr; Svietlieisha Olena/Shutterstock, 16bl; Africa Studio/Shutterstock, 16br.

Library of Congress Cataloging-in-Publication Data
Names: Nilsen, Genevieve, author.
Title: Oigo / por Genevieve Nilsen.
Other titles: Hear. Spanish
Description: Minneapolis: Jump!, Inc., (2023)
Series: Mis sentidos | Includes index.
Audience: Ages 3–6
Identifiers: LCCN 2022034662 (print)
LCCN 2022034663 (ebook)
ISBN 9798885242578 (hardcover)
ISBN 9798885242585 (paperback)
ISBN 9798885242592 (ebook)
Subjects: LCSH: Hearing—Juvenile literature.
Classification: LCC QP462.2 .N5518 2023 (print)
LCC QP462.2 (ebook)
DDC 612.8/5—dc23/eng/20220808

MIS SENTIDOS

OIGO

por Genevieve Nilsen

TABLA DE CONTENIDO

Palabras a saber 2

Oigo 3

¡Repasemos! 16

Índice 16

PALABRAS A SABER

cantando

estallando

ladrando

oigo

pitando

riéndose

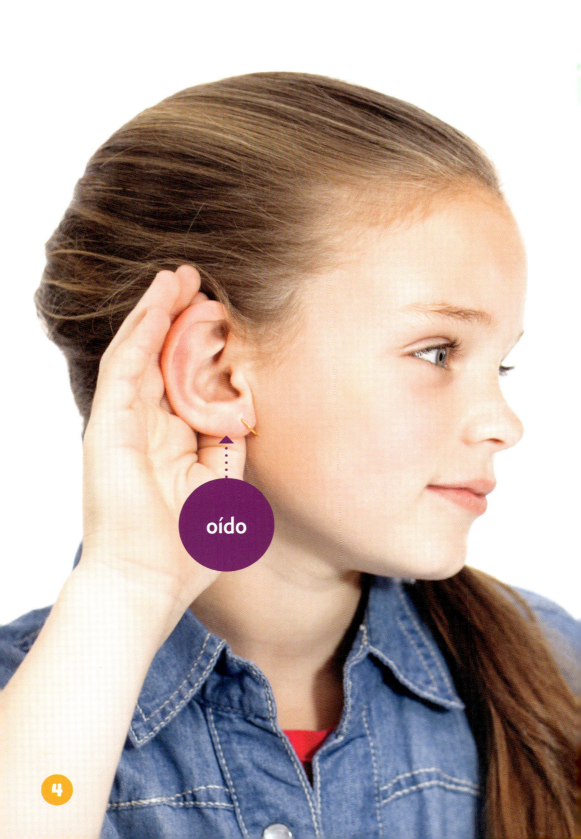

Oigo con los oídos.

Oigo a un pájaro cantando.

Oigo a un perro ladrando.

Oigo autos pitando.

Oigo olas estallando.

Oigo a amigos riéndose.

¡REPASEMOS!

Oímos sonidos con los oídos. ¿Qué sonidos hacen estas cosas y estos animales?

ÍNDICE

cantando 7
estallando 13
ladrando 9
oídos 5

oigo 3, 5, 7, 9, 11, 13, 15
pitando 11
riéndose 15
sonidos 3